Daily Affirmations For Women

365 Days of Positive, Empowering & Inspirational Affirmations
To Support Growth & Recovery

Emma Hyndall

Prologue

Firstly, I want to commend you on your pursuit of self-growth and recovery. Please recognize that you are doing an amazing job, and sincerely deserve everything this world has to offer.

While performing these affirmations, I encourage you to remain attentive to your current environment, and mindful of your presence.

Consider partaking in mindful breathing a few minutes before performing these affirmations to welcome a state of tranquility. A simple box breathing routine can inspire many health benefits, some of these include destressing our body and mind, improving mental clarity, and an increase in focus and energy levels. Just what you need for the day ahead, right?

To perform the box breathing exercise, start by breathing in through your nose to a relaxed count of four. Hold that breath at the peak for another four seconds. Next, begin to gradually exhale for an additional four seconds. Before finally sustaining an empty breath for a closing count of four. Repeat this exercise for several minutes or until you feel a sense of calm. This exercise can be implemented at any stage of the day.

If you would like to, journaling your thoughts and reflections during this time can be very beneficial. You may use these affirmations as prompts to spark thought trails that you can wander through while writing. It is a completely safe environment for you to express your concerns, your vulnerabilities, your gratitude, and your desires. You are not alone on this voyage of self-improvement. Understand that it will take time, and it will call on your honest self. However, becoming aware of what we are grateful for, or where we are in our lives gifts us with an amazing perspective to start repairing and building upon.

Now that you're ready, let's embark on this journey of healing!

Day 1

I breathe in confidence, and I exhale fear.

Day 2

I love and accept myself for who I am.

Day 3

I can handle anything life throws at me.

Day 4

Today is going to be wonderful, and full of happiness!

Day 5

I deserve kindness.

Day 6

I have the power to create change.

Day 7
I radiate confidence and positivity.

Day 8
I am grateful for my body.

Day 9
I am confident in my ability to help others.

Day 10
What I love about myself is my ability to dream.

Day 11
I find inspiration in the world around me.

Day 12
My strong work ethic helps me achieve my goals.

Day 13
I have complete faith in my intuition.

Day 14
I will raise my hand for opportunities that will help me grow.

Day 15
I trust myself to make the correct decision.

Day 16
I focus on the positive.

Day 17
I choose joy and comfort every day.

Day 18
I am thankful for my friends and family.

Day 19
The abundance of the universe is pouring into my life.

Day 20
Calmness washes over me with every breathe I take.

Day 21
Taking care of myself is productive.

Day 22
Wealth and prosperity are drawn to me.

Day 23
I am enough.

Day 24
I love that I can make others feel great.

Day 25

I am prepared, and I welcome all new challenges.

Day 26

I am excited for what the day brings.

Day 27

I am worthy.

Day 28

I grow exponentially every day.

Day 29

I am in the process of positive changes.

Day 30

I will focus on keeping a positive attitude while waiting.

Day 31
I gift myself permission to slow down.

Day 32
I trust in myself and my capability.

Day 33
I appreciate my surroundings.

Day 34
I am everything I desire to be.

Day 35
I am overflowing with infinite energy.

Day 36
I enjoy life to the fullest.

Day 37
I treat others with respect and appreciate their individuality.

Day 38
I value my time and input.

Day 39
I endeavor to be more open-minded.

Day 40
I look for fun and humor in as many situations as possible.

Day 41
I adore that I try new things.

Day 42

My body is healthy; my mind is brilliant; my soul is tranquil.

Day 43

I have developed many talents which I will utilize more.

Day 44

I possess the qualities needed to be extremely successful.

Day 45

I believe in myself and my ability to succeed.

Day 46

Creative energy surges through me and leads me to new and brilliant ideologies.

Day 47
My capacity to conquer challenges is limitless.

Day 48
I am courageous and very willing to stand up for myself and my values.

Day 49
I radiate beauty, charm, and grace.

Day 50
My life is just beginning.

Day 51
I wake up today with a courageous heart.

Day 52
I hold all the power I need within.

Day 53

I am disciplined and ready to accomplish anything I set my mind to.

Day 54

My perspective is unique and significant.

Day 55

I have blossomed into a beautiful, loving individual.

Day 56

Every ~~failure~~ I face is an opportunity for me to learn and grow.

Day 57

I truly believe in the person I am becoming.

Day 58
My soul is at peace.

Day 59
I am worthy of healing.

Day 60
I will embrace the glorious being that I am.

Day 61
I will say "no" when I do ~~not~~ have the time or inclination to act.

Day 62
I acknowledge my own self-worth; my confidence is soaring.

Day 63

I wake up each day inspired.

Day 64

I am a warrior, a fighter, and I will always persevere.

Day 65

Positivity is a choice; I choose to be positive.

Day 66

What I give is what I receive.

Day 67

I am loveable and loved.

Day 68

I am in harmony with the Universe, and it guides me effortlessly.

Day 69

I am noticing more vitality and beauty in my reflection.

Day 70

I deserve someone who adores me just as I am.

Day 71

I got this.

Day 72

Wonderful things are unravelling around me.

Day 73

I set clear goals and work to complete them every day.

Day 74
I receive all feedback with kindness but make the final call myself.

Day 75
I am the hero in my story.

Day 76
I am brave enough to climb any mountain or obstacle.

Day 77
My goals are my focus.

Day 78
I am gaining strength every day.

Day 79
I am doing my best, and that's okay.

Day 80

I will ~~not~~ worry about things I ~~cannot~~ control.

Day 81

I am sincerely grateful for all that I have.

Day 82

I am capable.

Day 83

I have the courage to pursue my dreams.

Day 84

The answer is right before me, even if I am ~~not~~ seeing it yet.

Day 85

I am safe and sound. All is well.

Day 86
I am comfortable in my own skin and will thrive in any environment.

Day 87
I adopt the mindset to praise myself more.

Day 88
I ~~cannot~~ give up until I have tried every possible outcome.

Day 89
I am deeply fulfilled with who I am.

Day 90
limiting beliefs have ~~no~~ power over me.

Day 91

I face the day with a sense tranquility and patience.

Day 92

I will be a giver of compassion today.

Day 93

All my ~~problems~~ have a solution.

Day 94

I'm grateful for adversity, because it allows me to grow.

Day 95

I am in charge of my own self-worth.

Day 96

I am surrounded by an abundance of opportunity.

Day 97

Success and happiness come easily to me.

Day 98

I transform anxiety into curiosity on my way to joy.

Day 99

Every day is a fresh start and new beginning.

Day 100

I am dedicated to building high self-esteem.

Day 101

I matter.

Day 102

I am super proud of myself.

Day 103
I stand up for what I believe in.

Day 104
I am open and ready to learn.

Day 105
Today is going to be an amazing day!

Day 106
The better I become, the better I attract.

Day 107
I am in alignment with my purpose.

Day 108
It is okay to ~~not~~ know everything.

Day 109
I am a magnet of wonder.

Day 110
I detach myself from ~~negativity~~.

Day 111
I celebrate my individuality.

Day 112
I am appreciative of where I am in my life.

Day 113
I trust myself.

Day 114
I choose to be compassionate.

Day 115
I am talented and intelligent.

Day 116
I am excited for what today will bring.

Day 117
I am a dazzling work of art.

Day 118
I am taking steps to make my dreams a reality.

Day 119
I release all ~~negative~~ energy.

Day 120
From now on everything I touch turns to gold.

Day 121
I welcome bliss into my life.

Day 122
It is perfectly okay to say "no" for my mental well-being.

Day 123
I commend every win, big or small.

Day 124
I've got my back.

Day 125
I commit to being happy.

Day 126

As I breathe in, I welcome new ideas, positive energies and feelings of growth.

Day 127

I encourage new ways of thinking.

Day 128

I'm <u>so</u> thankful for all the little things that put a smile on my face.

Day 129

I am an astounding listener and tremendous communicator.

Day 130

I love that I'm taking responsibility for my life and moving forward.

Day 131

I believe in what I deserve, therefor I will attract such.

Day 132

I am focused, persistent and will achieve great things.

Day 133

I can easily craft the life I desire.

Day 134

Where others see a challenge, I see opportunity.

Day 135

I will live with exuberance.

Day 136

I am ~~not~~ dependent on anyone else.

Day 137
I am calm, patient and in control of my emotions.

Day 138
The more I give, the more I shall I receive.

Day 139
I am happy, healthy and centered.

Day 140
I make a difference by showing up every day and giving my best.

Day 141
I will act after thought, not on instinct.

Day 142
Calm is my primary state of being.

Day 143
I am content.

Day 144
I feel strong, excited and powerful.

Day 145
I will work smarter, ~~not~~ harder.

Day 146
I will find the healthy balance between self-care and effort.

Day 147
I am ~~not~~ perfect, I am human.

Day 148
I have a voice, and that voice matters.

Day 149

I am equipped with all the tools required to succeed.

Day 150

I am kind hearted and bare a beautiful soul.

Day 151

I strive to be, the best version of me.

Day 152

I live in a universe where I am loved and supported.

Day 153

I'm at awe of what my body is capable of.

Day 154

I appreciate all that I have.

Day 155

I am at peace, because my intentions are good and my heart is pure.

Day 156

I release my mind of thought until the morning.

Day 157

I will ~~not~~ allow the words or actions of others to define how I view myself.

Day 158

My thoughts are my reality, so I bring forth a bright new day.

Day 159

I am in complete charge of my future.

Day 160

I feel profound empathy and love for others and their unique paths.

Day 161

I choose to focus my energy on empowerment.

Day 162

I believe in my ability to unravel the way and set myself free.

Day 163

I accept everyone as they are, and continue on pursuing my dream.

Day 164

Sometimes I ~~don't~~ know where I am going, but I will find my way eventually.

Day 165
I am resilient. I will bounce back.

Day 166
All of my decisions are inspired from inner wisdom and compassion.

Day 167
I am learning what I need to do to take care of my body and my mind.

Day 168
I am grateful for my ability to now manage my money well.

Day 169
My worth is untarnished by my imperfections of the way others see me.

Day 170

I am blessed beyond measure.

Day 171

I am dependable and resourceful.

Day 172

I am delighted with my recent efforts.

Day 173

I will stand back up every time I fall.

Day 174

Today, I surround myself with a bubble of peaceful energy.

Day 175

I am releasing myself from self-judgement.

Day 176
Wherever I go, I will move with self-confidence and conviction.

Day 177
I acknowledge my own self-worth.

Day 178
I hold responsibility for myself, ~~not~~ for anyone else.

Day 179
I have ~~nothing~~ to worry about.

Day 180
I am open to receiving more love in my life.

Day 181
By being myself, I bring happiness to others.

Day 182
I am tough and I can get through this.

Day 183
With each exhalation, I invite peace and serenity.

Day 184
Everything I need comes into my life at the right time.

Day 185
I am unstoppable.

Day 186
I belong here just as much as anybody else.

Day 187
My growth is a continuous process.

Day 188
I am letting go of all that ~~no~~ longer serves me.

Day 189
I deserve great things.

Day 190
I am capable of making substantial changes to my life.

Day 191
I am intrinsically motivated to achieve goals, overcome
challenges, and live with passion.

Day 192
I choose to stop apologizing for being myself.

Day 193
I am faithful in all of my endeavors.

Day 194

My body is sacred and I will take more care of it.

Day 195

I expect nothing, but appreciate everything.

Day 196

I shall start each day with a fresh perspective.

Day 197

The universe sends me admiration every day.

Day 198

Time is the essence of healing.

Day 199

I forgive myself for feeling anxious.

Day 200
I encourage space to breathe in the moment and recognize there is beauty in life's pauses.

Day 201
I'm still standing.

Day 202
I am thankful for my understanding of everything I'm going through.

Day 203
I need ~~nothing~~ more as I am content with less.

Day 204
I am creatively motivated by my surroundings.

Day 205

I wake up each morning feeling empowered.

Day 206

My body is relaxed and tranquil.

Day 207

I am a leader.

Day 208

I trust my judgement.

Day 209

I am kind and supportive to the reflection I see in the

mirror.

Day 210

I am on a journey, ever growing and developing.

Day 211
I protect myself against any hurt that comes my way.

Day 212
I am overflowing with energy.

Day 213
I give out respect and it is returned to me multiplied
manifold.

Day 214
I deserve to be healthy and feel remarkable!

Day 215
Happiness is my birthright.

Day 216
Good things are happening.

Day 217

I create a safe and secure space for myself
wherever I am.

Day 218

I treasure solitude, it will help me to decide the
direction I need to go.

Day 219

I am devoted to my spiritual growth.

Day 220

I allow the light of my consciousness to grow with
each and every day.

Day 221

Being alone gives me the chance to discover my inner
voice.

Day 222
I am deeply gratified by what I do.

Day 223
I honor my body by trusting the indicators that it
sends me.

Day 224
My thoughts become my reality.

Day 225
I am grounded in the experience of the present
moment.

Day 226
Angels watch over me.

Day 227

My heart knows my true path.

Day 228

I excel in everything I set my mind to.

Day 229

Success is always knocking at my door, I must simply open up to it.

Day 230

I am primed and ready to accept my dreams as reality.

Day 231

I stand with brilliant posture and vigor.

Day 232

I have amazing determination.

Day 233
It's okay for me to pursue everything I dream of.

Day 234
Something wonderful is about to happen to me.

Day 235
I organize my priorities with clarity.

Day 236
Good flows to me, good flows from me.

Day 237
I speak with certainty and calm assurance.

Day 238
I am in control of my reactions.

Day 239

Every life experience presents an opportunity to become wiser.

Day 240

I live my life with meaningful purpose.

Day 241

My will has ~~no~~ ceiling.

Day 242

I am filled with joy and pleasure to live another day.

Day 243

I will surprise myself.

Day 244

I am the architect of my surroundings.

Day 245
I enjoy working out, and I thrive off the energy it
gives me.

Day 246
I manifest perfect health by making smart decisions.

Day 247
I don't stop when I'm ~~tired~~, I stop when I am done.

Day 248
The time for change is now.

Day 249
Life has many lanes, I will be kind to myself, and to
others traversing in the same direction.

Day 250
I can and I will..

Day 251
I am ready to achieve greatness.

Day 252
I will organize and prioritize my time better.

Day 253
I promise to myself that I will embrace my feelings.

Day 254
My mind is a beautiful place.

Day 255
I develop innovative ideas.

Day 256

I recognize that I am worth a lot more than I first thought.

Day 257

I am brilliant and beautiful.

Day 258

Each day is a gift.

Day 259

I am a magnet for new and lasting friendships.

Day 260

I am brave, I am bold, I am strong.

Day 261

I love and respect myself deeply.

Day 262
I have faith in my skills and talents.

Day 263
I've discovered that I am fierce.

Day 264
Broken bridges will ~~not~~ hinder my momentum.

Day 265
I greet each day with thoughtfulness.

Day 266
My views and opinions are valuable.

Day 267
I am willing to receive support to get me through this
obstacle.

Day 268
I am emotionally able.

Day 269
I will follow my heart's desire.

Day 270
Nothing can stop me from feeling confident in who I have become!

Day 271
I have high self-esteem so I truly believe in my abilities.

Day 272
I am of high intellect and inspire many precious philosophies.

Day 273
Either it will work or it will not. I am eager to push forward either way.

Day 274
I will be stronger than my strongest excuse.

Day 275
I am a gigantic inspiration to those around me.

Day 276
I am letting go. I am free.

Day 277
I am protecting my joy.

Day 278
I am attracted to who I am becoming.

Day 279
I am a person of action.

Day 280
I am wise because I learn from my ~~mistakes~~.

Day 281
I am learning to love the feeling of walking away from things ~~not~~ meant for me.

Day 282
I am the ruler of my kingdom.

Day 283
I have decided now is the time to go for it.

Day 284
I can still love, and I still am loved.

Day 285

Once in a while something amazing comes along... and here I am.

Day 286

What I do today will make a difference tomorrow.

Day 287

I think, therefore I am.

Day 288

Life is tough, but I am tougher.

Day 289

I am enough, I have always been enough, I will always be enough.

Day 290
I have been through hell, so I know I have the strength to and drive to make it through anything.

Day 291
I love how independent I am.

Day 292
I can tap into a wellspring off inner joy and happiness anytime I wish.

Day 293
I am whole, I am worthy.

Day 294
I find pleasure in all of my endeavors, even the most mundane.

Day 295

I communicate my desires and needs clearly and confidently.

Day 296

I am becoming more and more efficient with each passing day.

Day 297

I personality exudes confidence. I am bold and outgoing.

Day 298

I have a contagious sense of humor and love to share laughter to those around me.

Day 299

I am immovable in my determination.

Day 300
I am as my creator made me and since he is content, so am I.

Day 301
By allowing myself to be happy, I inspire others to be happy as well.

Day 302
I am endlessly evolving.

Day 303
I have integrity, I am totally reliable, and I do what I say I will.

Day 304
Every cell in my body vibrates brilliance and positive energy.

Day 305

I send love and healing to every organ of my body.

Day 306

I sow the seeds of peace wherever I go.

Day 307

I am in the present moment and release the past to
live exclusively in the now.

Day 308

I welcome good things to happen in my life today.

Day 309

I am optimistic about my future.

Day 310

Life is simple, easy, and effortless.

Day 311
I am an outgoing person.

Day 312
I am my own muse.

Day 313
I am at peace and harmony with everyone and
everything.

Day 314
I let go of any past concerns and worries.

Day 315
I love meeting new and exciting people.

Day 316
In all that I say and do, I choose peace.

Day 317
I have ~~no~~ need to rush things, my time will come.

Day 318
I am impervious to doubt.

Day 319
I am resilient enough to recover from any tough situation.

Day 320
I gift myself permission to make choices.

Day 321
I continuously strive to improve my process.

Day 322
I am a responsible person and always get things completed on time.

Day 323
Persistence and consistency is my route to success.

Day 324
My mind is sharp and ready to take on whatever awaits.

Day 325
I am a highly efficient and disciplined person.

Day 326
Being organized allows me to do more in life.

Day 327
I have unlimited potential.

Day 328
Steadiness and ease are my natural state.

Day 329
I am exactly where I need to be right now.

Day 330
I am able to take on calculated risks if required
without fear.

Day 331
I am thankful for the opportunity to reconcile.

Day 332
I find joy in the most simple things in life.

Day 333
I have come so far from who I once was. Such a beautiful transition to witness.

Day 334
My passion is ready to find me.

Day 335
I am connected to the divine energy.

Day 336
I start each day with a grateful heart.

Day 337
I am attracted to people and situations that bring joy.

Day 338
My senses are heightened.

Day 339

I am driven by curiosity.

Day 340

I am beginning to trust the universe more.

Day 341

I put action into my words.

Day 342

No matter what happens today, I will stay positive and upbeat.

Day 343

I encourage success and prosperity.

Day 344

My mind is full of optimistic imageries.

Day 345

I make constructive choices towards staying fit.

Day 346

I am excited to go to work today.

Day 347

I am honored to be a part of something special.

Day 348

My inner self always has the answer.

Day 349

I have balance within me.

Day 350

I choose to be present in the now.

Day 351
I will be the reason someone feels welcomed, loved, heard, seen and supported today.

Day 352
I am practicing gratitude for everything I have daily.

Day 353
I bestow such a precious smile.

Day 354
I access my intuition easily and effortlessly.

Day 355
I am calming my body and destressing with every breath.

Day 356
I take pride in the work I do.

Day 357
living a creative life is important to me; it makes me a
healthier, happier person.

Day 358
I am a loyal, loving friend.

Day 359
I recognize how substantial it is to just listen to
others.

Day 360
I am attractive just as I am. I don't need to change
anything.

Day 361

I am respectful and entirely self-aware.

Day 362

The world craves more of what I have to offer.

Day 363

I look forward to feeling better about the universe again.

Day 364

My mental health is just as imperative as my physical health.

Day 365

There is nobody else in the world like me. That in itself is magical.

Epilogue

You made it! My sincerest compliments on your determination and resolve to see it through to the end. I hope you have reconciled with your inner-self and discovered you truly are a beautiful and honest soul.

Please refer back to this book any time you need any form of reassurance or healing.

Lastly, I send nothing but love and encouragement your way. Keep smiling girl, you got this!

If you liked this book, it would be sincerely appreciated if you could leave a review on Amazon. Let me know what you liked or even what you didn't like, as it helps me release better books in the future.
-Emma Hyndall

Printed in Great Britain
by Amazon

51230596R00047